GOD'S HEROES

OF THE BIBLE

Get ready to dive into ten incredible adventures starring courageous heroes straight from the pages of the Bible!

BY EVANGELIST JOAN PEARCE

Channel of Love Ministries

www.joanpearce.org

DEDICATED TO MY LOVING HUSBAND, MARTY

Channel of Love Ministries
www.joanpearce.org
PO Box 20069, Bradenton, FL 34204

God's Heroes
of the Bible
(ten short stories)

Written by Joan Pearce
Book design by Rebekah Zendzian

ISBN 978-1-958404-78-2

ADAM

GOD'S FALLEN HERO
(GENESIS 2:4-3:24)

IN THE VERY BEGINNING,

God made the whole wide world, the sky, the trees, the animals, and everything. He decided to create a special friend in His own image, so He made a man out of the dust and breathed life into him. The man was alive and had authority over all the animals. God loved spending time with the man, and they would chat in the cool of the day.

To keep the man company, God made a woman named Eve from one of the man's ribs. God gave them a big garden called Eden, and they could eat anything in the garden, except the fruit from one special tree: the tree of the knowledge of good and evil.

But one day, a sneaky serpent slithered into the garden. The serpent, who was actually Satan in disguise, whispered lies to Eve. He told her that if she ate from the forbidden tree, she would be like God, knowing everything.

Eve listened to the serpent's tempting words, and she began to desire the fruit from the forbidden tree. She imagined herself being as wise and powerful as God. So, sadly, she took a bite of the fruit and gave some to Adam too.

As soon as they disobeyed God's command, something changed. They felt a deep sadness and fear creeping into their hearts. They realized they had made a terrible mistake. Their disobedience brought a consequence—they were separated from the loving presence of God. They became mortal, subject to sickness, pain, and death.

Have you ever wondered why bad things happen in the world if God is good? It's a big question, but the Bible helps us understand. It all started when Adam and Eve disobeyed God.

That's when everything got messed up, like when a computer gets a virus and doesn't work right. Because of Adam and Eve's mistake, the entire world was put under a curse. But God did not abandon His creation. He had a plan—a plan of love and redemption...

Now, Adam could have been a hero if he chose to walk with God. If he had listened to God's instructions and resisted the temptation of the serpent, he could have helped Eve make the right choice. He could have been a strong leader, guiding his family with wisdom and love.

Despite their mistake, Adam and Eve's story teaches us important lessons. It reminds us to listen to God's words and make good choices. It also shows us the power of forgiveness and the hope of redemption from the ultimate hero that was to come—Jesus, the Son of God.

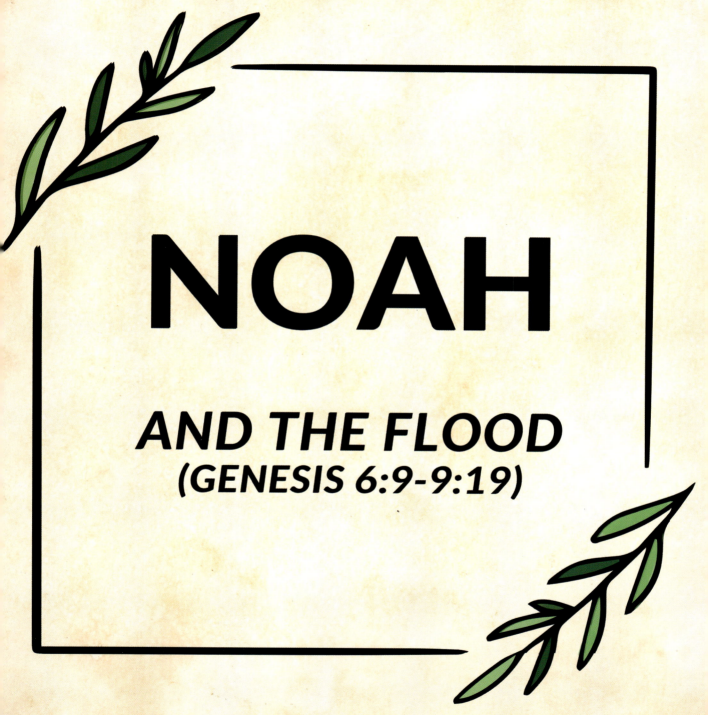

NOAH

AND THE FLOOD
(GENESIS 6:9-9:19)

LONG AGO,

when the world was beginning to fill up with lots of people, things weren't going very well. People were not kind to each other; they were doing things that made God very sad. He looked down from the heavens and wished he hadn't made mankind at all. But in the midst of this darkness, there was one man who shone brightly in God's eyes – Noah.

God decided to share his plan with Noah. He said, "Noah, I have seen your pure heart. I want you to build a special boat, an ark made of gopherwood. I am going to send a great flood to wash away the wickedness, and you and your family, along with two of every animal, will be saved on the ark."

Noah, being a man of righteousness, didn't hesitate. He gathered wood and tools and started working on the ark. As he worked tirelessly, his neighbors, who had never seen rain before, found the idea amusing. They laughed and made fun of Noah, wondering why he was building such a huge boat on dry land.

But Noah didn't let their mocking bother him. He knew he had to follow God's instructions. Meanwhile, God shared his plan with the animals. Giraffes, elephants, birds of all kinds – they all started their journey to Noah's ark.

As the ark took shape, the whispers of the coming rain grew louder. Dark clouds gathered in the sky, and suddenly, raindrops began to fall. The people who had mocked Noah now panicked, but it was too late. God had closed the door of the ark, sealing Noah, his family, and the animals inside.

The rain turned into a mighty downpour, and the earth trembled as the waters below burst open, covering everything. Days passed, and the rain continued relentlessly. The ark floated above the flooded world, keeping its inhabitants safe.

Finally, after forty days and nights, the rain stopped. Noah, his family, and the animals waited patiently inside the ark. As the water slowly receded, the ark settled on solid ground. God kept his promise, and the first thing Noah saw when he opened the ark's door was a magnificent rainbow stretching across the sky.

God spoke to Noah and said, "I promise never to destroy the world again with a flood. Whenever you see a rainbow, remember our covenant – a special agreement between us. It's a sign of my love and promise to never flood the world again."

Noah and his family thanked God for keeping them safe. From that day forward, whenever rain fell and a rainbow appeared, they remembered the importance of obeying God and staying close to Him. The colorful arc in the sky was a reminder of hope, love, and the enduring promise of a brighter tomorrow. And so, the story of Noah and the ark became a beacon of light in the history of the world.

MOSES

AND THE ISRAELITES
(EXODUS)

A LONG TIME AGO,

in a faraway place called Egypt, there was a little baby named Moses. He was an Israelite, which means he was part of God's special group of people. But Moses had a big problem – the ruler of Egypt, Pharaoh, was being unkind to the Israelites. Pharaoh even said all baby boys like Moses had to be killed.

But guess what? Moses' mom and sister didn't want anything bad to happen to him. So, they put Moses in a special basket and let him float down a river. Pharaoh's daughter found him and said, "Oh, this baby is so cute! I'll take care of him." So, Moses grew up in Pharaoh's palace, like an Egyptian prince!

When Moses became a grownup, he saw the Israelites working so hard, and he wanted to help them. But he didn't listen to God and did things his own way, and he got into a lot of trouble.

He ran away from Pharaoh's castle and his people into the desert.

Many years later, God talked to him through a burning bush in the desert and said, "Moses, you're going to lead the Israelites out of Egypt to a better place!"

But Moses felt scared and unsure. He didn't think he was good at speaking, and he worried that he might not do a good job. So, Moses asked God if someone else could go with him to talk to the Pharaoh.

God allowed Moses' brother, Aaron, to help him.

Moses went to Pharaoh and said, "Let my people go!" But Pharaoh said no. So, God sent terrible events called plagues to show Pharaoh how powerful He was.

There were frogs, bugs, and even a big sea turning into blood! But Pharaoh still said no.

Then came the last and scariest plague. The angel of death would visit every house in Egypt, but God told the Israelites to paint the blood of a lamb on their doors. This way, the angel of death would know to pass by their homes. It worked, and the Israelites were safe!

This event was like a preview or foreshadowing of something special that would happen later. Just like the blood protected the Israelites, Jesus, who is called the Lamb of God, would shed His blood to save everyone from sin and death.

So, when we see the blood on the doors in this Bible story, it reminds us of how Jesus' blood protects us and saves us from harm. It shows us that God always has a plan to keep us safe and bring us to a better place.

Pharaoh finally agreed and the Israelites dashed out of Egypt in excitement. God worked a fantastic miracle by parting a huge sea, creating a dry road for them to walk on safely. But then, Pharaoh's army tried to chase them, only to see the sea crash back, keeping the Israelites out of harm's way.

Next, as the Israelites journeyed through the desert toward their promised land, Moses led the way. During the day, a special cloud from God shielded them from the scorching sun, and at night, a bright fire lit their path. Even though the desert was hot and dry, God provided them with supernatural food called manna and fresh water to drink.

The Israelites' desert journey was filled with delays because sometimes they didn't listen to God, choosing their own ways instead. God gave Moses ten important rules called the Ten Commandments. These rules were like a special guidebook, teaching the Israelites how to love God and each other.

Despite facing challenges, they eventually arrived in the beautiful land of Canaan with God's help. Sadly, Moses couldn't enter Canaan because of mistakes he made. Yet, God picked Joshua and Caleb to lead the people into Canaan, just as He promised.

Even though Moses couldn't go to the promised land, he was still a hero to the Israelites because of his strong faith in God and his leadership. This shows us that no matter our insecurities or fears, we can be brave knowing that God will be our strength, just like He was for Moses.

JOSHUA

AND THE WALLS OF JERICHO
(JOSHUA 6:1–27)

AFTER MOSES,

Joshua led the Israelites with bravery. God said to him, "Go, take over Canaan. Everywhere you walk, it's yours!" Their first challenge was Jericho, a city with giant walls. But God had a secret plan. He said, "March around Jericho once a day for six days. On the seventh day, march around seven times and then shout!" Joshua believed God and did just as he was told.

They circled Jericho, with priests carrying the special Ark of the Covenant (where God's presence was) and blowing trumpets. When Joshua and the army shouted on the seventh round, something amazing happened! The walls crashed down to the ground! What a huge victory it was!

You know why? Because God had sent angels to help Joshua in the battle. These angels were like superheroes, fighting for Joshua and the Israelites. God will always be there for you too, just like He was for Joshua. So, whenever you face tough times, remember that God has angels on a special mission to protect you and help you in every battle of life.

DAVID was a shepherd boy that the prophet of God anointed to be the new king of Israel. He wasn't a king yet, but God had big plans for him.

One day, David's brothers were in a big battle, and David went to bring them lunch. That's when he saw a giant named Goliath, who was as tall as a tree and twice as wide!

Goliath was saying mean things about God, and David couldn't believe it. "You can't talk about my God like that!" he thought. David remembered how God helped him fight lions and bears when he was taking care of his sheep. So, he picked up some smooth stones and put them in his sling.

With a brave heart, David ran toward Goliath. He swung his sling, and one of the stones hit Goliath right on the head! Goliath fell down, and the whole land cheered because David trusted God and became a hero.

Later on, God made David the king of Israel! So, whenever you face big challenges, remember David, the shepherd boy who became a king because he trusted God. Be strong in God, and you can be a hero too! Always stay close to God, and you'll see how amazing you can be!

THE 3 HEBREW BOYS

AND THE FIERY FURNACE
(DANIEL 3:8-30)

IN THE ANCIENT LAND OF BABYLON,

there were three friends named Shadrach, Meshach, and Abednego. They loved God a lot. But one day, their king named Nebuchadnezzar wanted everyone to worship his golden statue and not God. But Shadrach, Meshach, and Abednego knew it was wrong to worship any statue, so they said, "No way! We only worship God." This made the king very angry. He ordered them to bow down to his statue, or else they would be thrown into a hot, fiery furnace.

Guess what happened inside the furnace? Shadrach, Meshach, and Abednego weren't alone! There was a fourth person with them. It was Jesus! They danced around in the fiery furnace, and guess what? They didn't get burned at all! In fact, when they walked out of the fire, they didn't even smell like smoke.

This story teaches us that just like Shadrach, Meshach, and Abednego, we should never give up on worshiping and believing in God, even if it's hard. In our modern times, we might face challenges where people want us to believe or do things that go against our faith. But just like these brave friends, we should stand strong and not compromise what we know is right. God will always be with us, even in the tough times, just like He was with Shadrach, Meshach, and Abednego in the fiery furnace!

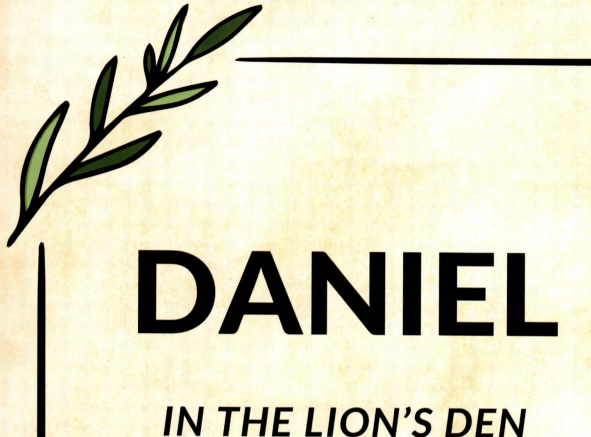

DANIEL

IN THE LION'S DEN
(DANIEL 6)

IN A FARAWAY LAND,

there was a man named Daniel who loved God a whole lot. He was really excellent at everything he did! Now, there were some other people who worked with Daniel, but they weren't happy. They got super jealous because Daniel was so good at his job, and everyone liked him.

One day, these not-so-nice people tricked the king into making a rule. They said, "Make a rule that if anyone prays to their God instead of you, they should be thrown into a den of hungry lions." The king didn't know they were talking about Daniel, so he agreed.

But guess what? Daniel loved God so much that he didn't stop praying, even when he knew about the new rule. He prayed just like he always did, thanking God and talking to Him.

The jealous people saw Daniel praying, and they told the king. The king felt really sad because he liked Daniel, but he had to follow the rule. So, they put Daniel in the lion's den.

But here's the amazing part - God sent an angel to shut the lions' mouths! He was safe all night!

The next morning, the king ran to the lion's den and called out, "Daniel, did your God save you?" And Daniel said, "Yes! God sent an angel, and the lions didn't even touch me."

The king realized how special Daniel was. Those jealous people, though, got what they planned for Daniel. They were thrown into the lion's den, and it didn't go well for them.

This story teaches us that when we love and trust God, He protects us, just like He did for Daniel.

JONAH

AND THE WHALE
(JONAH 1-3)

A LONG TIME AGO,

there was a man named Jonah, and he loved God. One day, God told Jonah, "I want you to go to the city of Nineveh and tell the people to stop doing wrong things."

But Jonah didn't want to go to Nineveh. He didn't like the people there, and he thought they were making too many mistakes. So instead of doing what God said, Jonah hopped on a boat going in the opposite direction. He wanted to run away from what God asked him to do.

While Jonah was on the boat, a big storm came, and the sailors got really scared. They found out it was because Jonah was running away from God's plan. Jonah told them to throw him into the sea to stop the storm, and when they did, a huge fish, like a whale, came and swallowed Jonah up!

Inside the fish, Jonah realized he should have listened to God. He prayed and said, "I'm sorry, God. I'll do what you asked." So, after three days and nights, the fish spat Jonah out on the shore.

This time, Jonah decided to obey God. He went to Nineveh and told the people about God. Surprisingly, the people of Nineveh listened, and they stopped doing wrong things. God was happy because they changed their ways.

The story of Jonah teaches us that we should always obey God, even when it's hard or we don't understand. God loves everyone, and He wants us to tell others about His love, just like Jonah did for the people of Nineveh. Today, it's like telling our friends and family about Jesus. We should want to share the good news and help others know God's love!

MARY

AND THE MIRACULOUS BIRTH OF JESUS
(LUKE 1:26-2:21)

LONG AGO, in a town named Nazareth, there lived a girl named Mary. She was kind and loved God very much. One day, an angel named Gabriel appeared before her. "Mary," he said with a smile, "God has a special plan for you! You're going to be the mom of the Savior, the one who will bring joy to the world!"

Mary blinked in surprise. She was just a young girl, after all. But the angel reassured her, saying, "Don't be afraid, Mary. God will be with you every step of the way." And Mary, with a brave heart, replied, "I will do whatever God wants."

Now, this was going to be no ordinary birth. It was a miracle! You see, Jesus was not going to be born like other babies. He was conceived by the power of the Holy Spirit, a gift from God himself.

Soon, Mary and her husband Joseph had to go to Bethlehem. It was a long journey, and when they arrived, there was no room for them in the inn. So, they found shelter in a stable, where Mary gave birth to a baby boy and named him Jesus.

That night, as Jesus lay in a manger, surrounded by animals, the sky lit up with bright stars. Angels appeared to shepherds nearby, telling them the wonderful news about the baby who would change the world.

Mary may not have been a queen or a princess, but she was chosen by God because of her pure and loving heart. And just like Mary, each one of us has a special place in God's plan.

So remember, no matter how small or ordinary you may feel, God has a purpose for you. Like Mary, you can say, "I am ready to do what God wants." And with that simple act of faith, you too can be part of something truly amazing in God's big and wonderful plan!

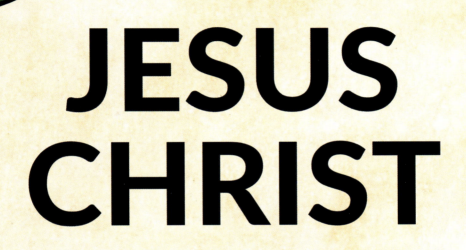

JESUS CHRIST

OUR ULTIMATE HERO!
(THE GOSPEL OF JOHN)

NOW, LET'S TALK ABOUT THE GREATEST HERO EVER—JESUS!

He isn't just a hero; He is God's Son, and He came to save the whole world!

Jesus showed us love and kindness, and He taught us how to be good. He is fully God and fully man and came to live life here on earth just like we do, but he never sinned.

He did many miracles, including healing sick people of all their diseases. But some people didn't understand Him, and they made a really bad choice. They put Jesus on a cross. It was very painful, and Jesus felt a lot of hurt.

On that cross, Jesus took away all the wrong things we do. It's like He cleaned our hearts and made us new. Then, after three days, something super special happened – Jesus came back to life! He defeated sin and death, and that's why He is the greatest hero of all.

Now, Jesus has an awesome plan for your life. He wants to be your friend and help you every day. All you have to do is talk to Him. You can say:

"Jesus, I'm sorry for the wrong things I've done. Thank you for forgiving me. I want to follow you and make you my Lord. Come into my heart and be my friend forever."

When you ask Jesus to be your Lord, it's like having a superhero in your heart who will always love and protect you.

So, if you want Jesus to be your friend and your Savior, just say that special prayer and commit to follow what Jesus teaches us in the Bible, and you'll be a part of His amazing plan!

God promises His people that one day, He will make everything new! He will create a new heaven and a new earth where there will be no more bad stuff like sickness or sadness. It will be like a perfect party with God and all His friends!

God wants everyone to be part of His big, happy family, but it's up to each person to choose to follow Him. God gave us something super special called free will, which means we can decide what we believe and how we want to live.

As we follow God and keep Jesus in our hearts, we can be heroes too! We can share joy and tell others about Jesus' love and the good news of God's kingdom. It's exciting to know that God's love is with us every day and that an amazing future is waiting for us when we believe.

Revelation 21:1-4 Then I saw a new heaven and a new earth, for the old heaven and the old earth had disappeared. And the sea was also gone. 2 And I saw the holy city, the new Jerusalem, coming down from God out of heaven like a bride beautifully dressed for her husband. 3 I heard a loud shout from the throne, saying, "Look, God's home is now among his people! He will live with them, and they will be his people. God himself will be with them. 4 He will wipe every tear from their eyes, and there will be no more death or sorrow or crying or pain. All these things are gone forever."

My name is:

_____

The name of my church is:

_____

On this date, I decided to follow Jesus:

_____

On this date, I was baptized in water:

_____

Acts 2:38-39 NLT Peter replied, "Repent and be baptized, every one of you, in the name of Jesus Christ for the forgiveness of your sins. And you will receive the gift of the Holy Spirit. 39 The promise is for you and your children and for all who are far off—for all whom the Lord our God will call."

EVANGELIST JOAN PEARCE'S LIFE is a captivating narrative of divine intervention, unwavering faith, and tireless dedication to spreading God's love. Her journey began with a profound conversion experience in 1977, a moment that ignited a passion for ministry that continues to burn brightly today.

After her conversion, Joan found herself in the picturesque landscapes of Washington State, where she encountered mentors who would shape her spiritual journey. Inspired and mentored by the daughter and son-in-law of the late Evangelist John G. Lake, Joan's faith was strengthened, and she received a clear calling from God to lead Bible studies despite her initial inability to read. This marked the beginning of a remarkable journey of faith where Joan recognized God's guiding hand and embraced her destiny in ministry.

Joan's heart resonates with the mission outlined in Luke 4:18–19—to bring the message of hope to the poor, heal the brokenhearted, and offer freedom to the oppressed. This mission fuels her passion for souls and drives her to proclaim the transformative power of God's love wherever she goes.

Since committing to full-time ministry in 1983, Joan, alongside her husband Marty, has traversed continents, bringing revival and renewal to communities worldwide. Their impactful "God is Taking the City" campaigns unite churches in a shared mission to evangelize cities, fostering unity and spiritual growth.

Their ministry extends beyond traditional evangelism to practical outreach, including feeding and clothing the needy, reflecting God's love in tangible ways. Joan and Marty's Holy Spirit Miracle Services are marked by notable miracles, showcasing the supernatural power of God at work in people's lives.

With a global reach through international TV broadcasts, Joan spreads her message of hope and salvation across the United States via www.wbntv.org. Together, Joan and Marty embody the essence of the Great Commission, passionately fulfilling the mandate to "Go into all the world and preach the gospel" (Mark 16:15).

www.joanpearce.org